Me and my Pony

By Kate Fordham

Put your favorite pony picture in this box.

With thanks to Nick Page, Helen Parker, and Lene Holmen.

Scholastic and Tangerine Press and associated logos are trademarks of Scholastic Inc.

Published by Tangerine Press, an imprint of Scholastic Inc., 557 Broadway, New York, NY 10012

10 9 8 7 6 5 4 3 2 1
ISBN-10 0-545-02110-3
ISBN-13 978-0-545-02110-4
Printed and bound in China

Scholastic Canada   Scholastic Australia Pty. Ltd
Markham, Ontario   Gosford, NSW

Scholastic New Zealand   Scholastic UK
Greenmount, Auckland   Coventry, Warwickshire

Copyright © 2007
make believe ideas ltd
27 Castle Street, Berkhamsted, Herts, HP4 2DW

What pony is right for you?

What kind of pony owner are you?
Want to find the perfect pony for you? Well, let's first find out what kind of person you are!

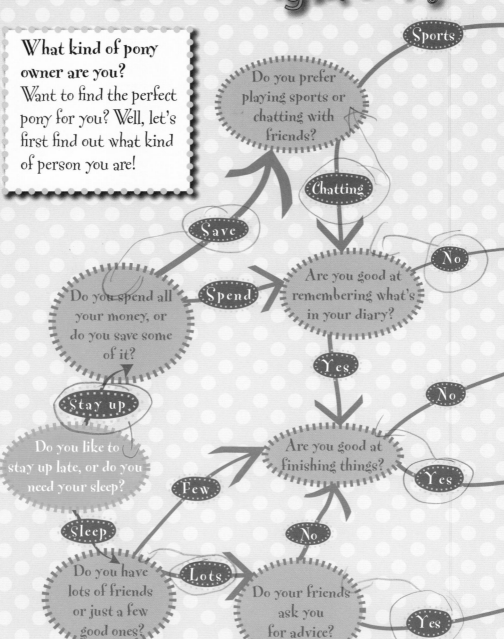

Sports

Do you prefer playing sports or chatting with friends?

Chatting

Save

No

Do you spend all your money, or do you save some of it?

Spend

Are you good at remembering what's in your diary?

Yes

No

Stay up

No

Do you like to stay up late, or do you need your sleep?

Few

Are you good at finishing things?

Yes

Sleep

No

Do you have lots of friends or just a few good ones?

Lots

Do your friends ask you for advice?

Yes

Do you know exactly what you want for your birthday? Or do you change your mind a lot?

Know exactly

When you play with friends, do they follow your ideas?

No

Change your mind

YES

Do you get in trouble for talking too much at school?

You're watching an exciting movie. Do you find it hard to sit still?

No

Party

At the fair do you go on the scary rides?

Do you prefer going to a party or staying in with a good book?

Book

No

Action

Do you like action movies or romances?

Romance

NO

Do you like taking care of babies and young children?

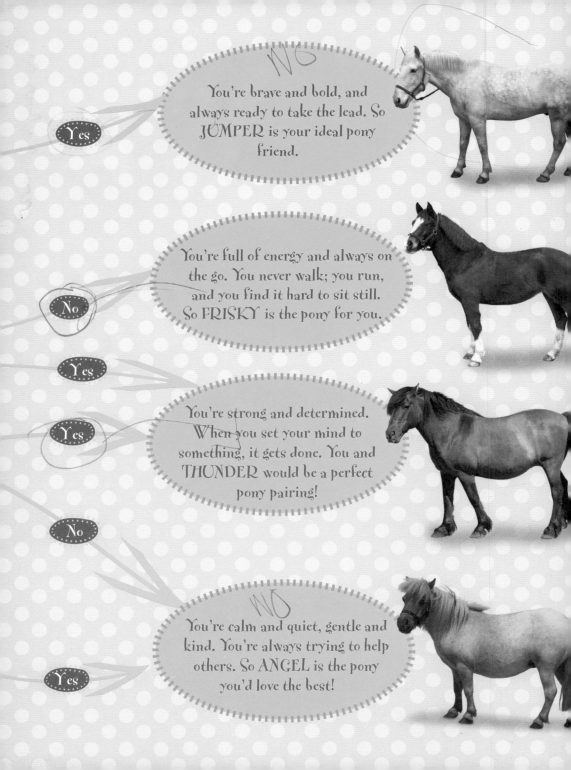

Yes

You're brave and bold, and always ready to take the lead. So JUMPER is your ideal pony friend.

No

You're full of energy and always on the go. You never walk; you run, and you find it hard to sit still. So FRISKY is the pony for you.

Yes

Yes

You're strong and determined. When you set your mind to something, it gets done. You and THUNDER would be a perfect pony pairing!

No

You're calm and quiet, gentle and kind. You're always trying to help others. So ANGEL is the pony you'd love the best!

Yes

Choosing a Pony

So you want a pony?

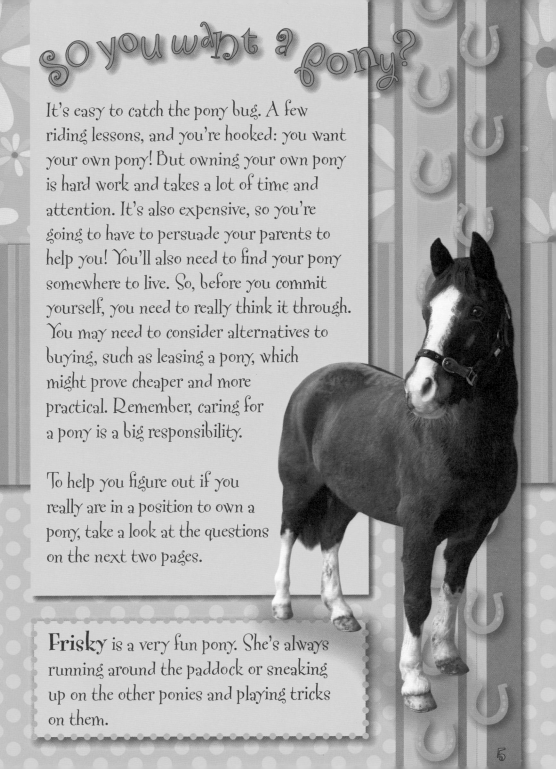

It's easy to catch the pony bug. A few riding lessons, and you're hooked: you want your own pony! But owning your own pony is hard work and takes a lot of time and attention. It's also expensive, so you're going to have to persuade your parents to help you! You'll also need to find your pony somewhere to live. So, before you commit yourself, you need to really think it through. You may need to consider alternatives to buying, such as leasing a pony, which might prove cheaper and more practical. Remember, caring for a pony is a big responsibility.

To help you figure out if you really are in a position to own a pony, take a look at the questions on the next two pages.

Frisky is a very fun pony. She's always running around the paddock or sneaking up on the other ponies and playing tricks on them.

Some really important questions

1. Can you afford a pony?
A pony costs a lot of money to buy and also to take care of. You will need money to pay for stabling, buying tack and equipment, food, and medical care.

2. Do you have the time?
Just as important as money: do you have the time you need to look after a pony? Ponies need a lot of care and attention.

3. Can you house a pony?
Do you have a field where your pony can live? Or will you have to pay to stable a pony elsewhere? If you do have enough space, is there a shelter to protect your pony from the wind and rain?

4. Are you prepared to get dirty?
You will get dirty looking after a pony. The stable needs to be mucked out and your pony cleaned and groomed in all weather.
It's hard, dirty, time-consuming work.

5. Do you have some help?

Who will look after your pony when you are away? Who will make sure that your pony is fed and watered and exercised?

6. Do you have the equipment you need?

You need lots of special, and often expensive, equipment to ride and care for a pony, as well as safe riding gear for yourself.

7. Do you have any experience with ponies?

Are you taking riding lessons? Do you stay to help out at the stables? Have you ever tried your hand at grooming a pony?

8. Do you have transportation for your pony?

If you plan to enter shows and gymkhanas with your pony, you will need a horse trailer and driver to transport it to competitions!

If the answer to these questions is "YES," then maybe – just maybe – you could be ready to have your very own pony.

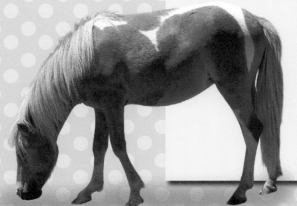

persuading your parents

You might have decided that buying a pony is right for you – but how are you going to pay for it? The best people to ask for help are probably your parents. But first, you need to convince them that it is a good idea and that you're serious. You might manage to convince them overnight, but it could take weeks or even months before they see your point of view. Here are just a few things you could try!

Start by talking

- Tell your parents how much you want a pony and prove to them that you understand that it'll be lots of time and work. Convince them owning a pony is not a whim and that you are capable of being a responsible and safe horse owner.

Be prepared to compromise

- If you live in a town or if your parents do not have enough money, you may need to discuss alternatives to buying a pony (see page 15).

Be realistic

- Don't expect your parents to just hand over a wad of cash for you to go out and spend. Prove to them that you understand that owning a horse is expensive. Show them you realize that the price of the horse itself is small compared with the cost of food, stabling, shoeing, and vets' fees. Think up ways you could help to raise money.

Be prepared to make sacrifices

- Are you willing to give up new clothes and treats so you can have a pony?

Keep it up

- Once you've convinced your parents to let you have a pony, your work isn't over. Your job now will be to look after your pony and continue to prove to your parents that buying you a pony was a good idea.

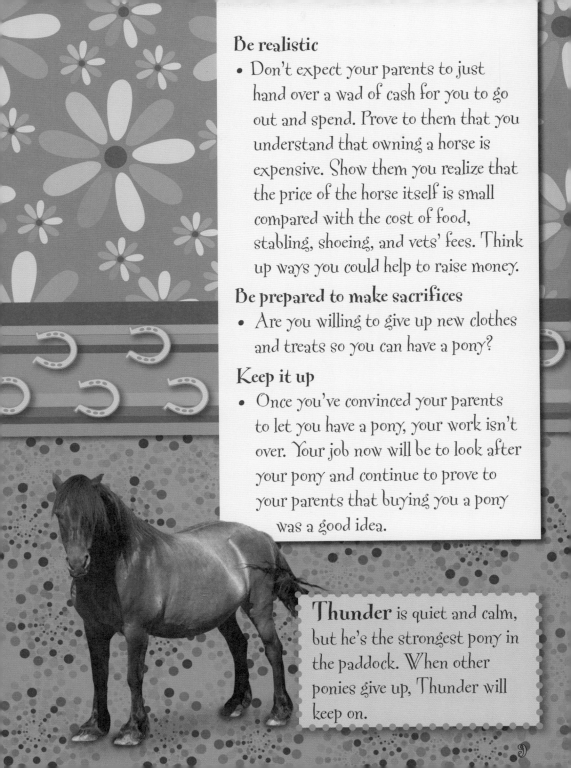

Thunder is quiet and calm, but he's the strongest pony in the paddock. When other ponies give up, Thunder will keep on.

Choosing a pony

Buying a pony is a big responsibility, so be sure to choose one that is suited to you and your experience as a rider. The last thing you want is a pony that you can't ride.

- **Ask for advice.** An experienced rider, such as your instructor, will be able to help you choose the right pony for you.

- **Choose the right size.** Ideally, you should be able to mount from the ground. Once mounted, your feet should not dangle below the pony's tummy.

- **What sort of a rider are you?** If you have only just started riding or only plan to go for easy weekend rides, look for a quiet pony. But if you intend to use your pony for competitions, you will need a fit pony with lots of energy.

TOP TIP

If you are buying your first pony, it is a good idea to attend a pony-care course before starting to look. Better still, get a parent to go with you!

10

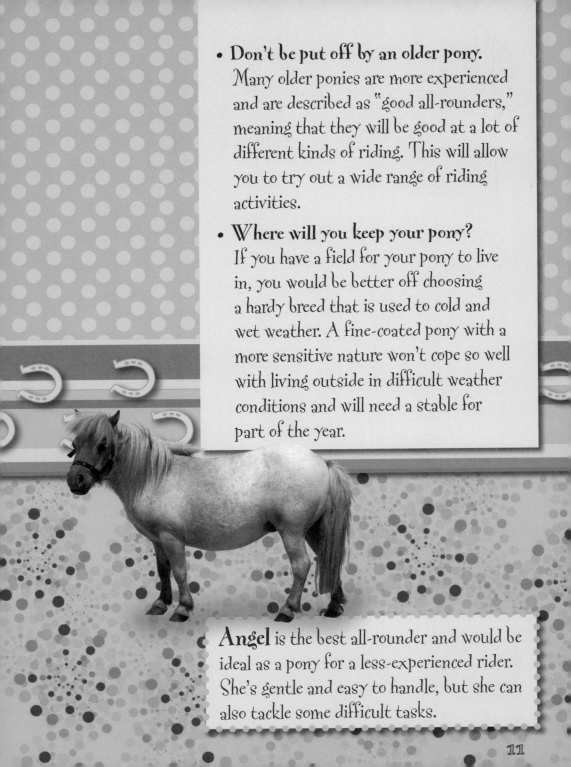

- **Don't be put off by an older pony.** Many older ponies are more experienced and are described as "good all-rounders," meaning that they will be good at a lot of different kinds of riding. This will allow you to try out a wide range of riding activities.

- **Where will you keep your pony?** If you have a field for your pony to live in, you would be better off choosing a hardy breed that is used to cold and wet weather. A fine-coated pony with a more sensitive nature won't cope so well with living outside in difficult weather conditions and will need a stable for part of the year.

Angel is the best all-rounder and would be ideal as a pony for a less-experienced rider. She's gentle and easy to handle, but she can also tackle some difficult tasks.

Kinds of Ponies

There are many different breeds of ponies to choose from, each with their own distinctive characteristics. They may be good jumpers, docile riding ponies, strong for pulling a cart, or sure-footed and steady for long-distance trail rides. It's worth taking some time to look up breeds in books and on specialist websites (with a parent) to find one that suits your needs.

When looking for a pony, you also need to take into account its age, level of training, and, very importantly, its personality!

Jumper is the leader of the gang – the Prince of the Paddock. He always wants to win!

PONY FACT

The Shetland is the smallest pony breed. It originally comes from the remote Shetland islands in northern Scotland. Today, there are Shetland ponies all over the world.

What color should I choose?

Ponies come in a wide range of colors. In some, the legs, mane, and tail may be a different color from the body. Which is your favorite?

Sorrel or chestnut – reddish brown, with a reddish-brown mane and tail.

Bay – brown, with black legs, mane, and tail.

Brown – very dark brown with black mane and tail.

White – pink skin and pink or blue eyes.

Pinto – white with large patches of another color.

PONY FACT

Pinto ponies were used by buffalo hunters on the American Great Plains. The word "pinto" means painted in Spanish.

Gray – born dark, with dark skin. Gets lighter with age. May be pure gray or dappled gray.

Black – very dark, with some brown highlights.

Dun – sandy yellow, with a dark mane and tail.

Palomino – golden body, with a white mane and tail.

Roan – mixture of white hairs with chestnut, bay, or black. Strawberry roan is chestnut and white. Blue roan is black and white.

PONY FACT

Queen Isabella of Spain loved palomino horses. The Spanish conquistador Hernando Cortés took the first palominos to the American continent in 1519.

Alternatives to buying

If you're desperate for a pony, but buying one is out of the question, consider some of the following:

Leasing Some owners lend ponies to other people in return for money. You don't buy the pony, but you still have to pay for its food, care, and stabling. Make sure you get a proper written agreement.

Pony clubs Joining a pony club is a great way to learn about pony care. You often don't have to own a pony to be a member.

Pony camps In summer, many pony clubs organize pony camps, which are fun ways to learn about ponies. Look in pony magazines to find out what's coming up.

TOP TIP

Go online with a parent to look for samples of written agreements for buying and leasing a pony.

Buying your pony

So, you're ready to buy your pony. You have a good idea of the kind of pony you would like, you're doing well in your riding lessons, you've found somewhere for your pony to live, and you're ready to buy the equipment you'll need. The next step is to find who has a pony for sale.

Where to look
- local newspapers
- bulletin boards in stables and tack shops
- horse and pony magazines
- Internet sites with classified web pages

Look locally. It's always more practical if you can find a pony that's for sale locally. This makes it easier to visit the pony before you buy. And, if you decide to go ahead, transportation is not as much of a problem.

TOP TIP
Always seek the help and advice of an experienced rider. He or she will help you to make a good choice of pony.

Try out the pony yourself. Never buy a pony that you haven't ridden and handled. You need to know if it's frisky in the stable or impossible to catch in the field. Ask the person selling the pony to ride it first so that you can have a good look at it.

Be informed. Get details of the pony's history and any illnesses or injuries it might have had.

Get a veterinary report. Before you buy a pony, always ask a vet to examine it and produce a report on its health. You may not be able to insure your pony without this. Obviously, this is no guarantee your pony won't get injured, but it should pick up any obvious faults or problems.

Get the paperwork. Make sure you put all the details of the sale in a proper written agreement. Check also that you have:
- your pony's passport
- vaccination records
- breed certificate, if applicable

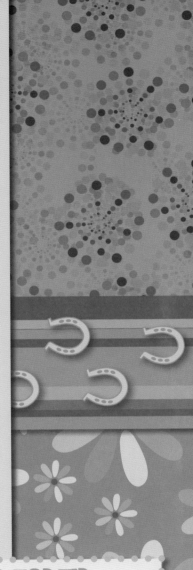

TOP TIP

Ponies cost a lot of money, so it's wise to insure them against theft and injury.

Quick Quiz

How wild about ponies are you?

To have a pony, you've got to be wild about them! So, here's a quick quiz to test how enthusiastic about ponies you really are!

Circle Yes or No for each statement:

I'm always dreaming about riding a pony. YES/NO

I don't mind getting dirty and mucking out a stall. YES/NO

I love to pretend to ride and gallop around the house. YES/NO

I'd rather have a pony than new clothes and exotic vacations. YES/NO

My room is full of pictures of ponies. YES/NO

My shelves are full of model horses. YES/NO

Riding is my favorite hobby. YES/NO

My favorite place in the world is the stables. YES/NO

I'd really enjoy getting up early to feed a pony. YES/NO

When I watch a movie, I look at the horses and not the actors. YES/NO

How many "yes" answers did you circle?

All 10 — Wow! There's no doubt about it – you're pony wild! Good thing you've got this book.

7–9 — Great! You may not be pony wild, but you're really into ponies.

4–6 — You still have a little ways to go before you have your own pony. Try spending more time at the stables and see what you're missing out on!

1–3 — Well, you're a bit interested, but you'll need to be a lot more excited if you're going to have a pony of your own!

What equipment do I need?

What equipment do I need?

You need lots of equipment to look after a pony. So, be prepared! Stock up on supplies before you bring your pony home. You can buy most equipment from saddlers, livery stores, or specialist online stores. However, you will not be able to buy a lot of the tack you need until after you have your pony. Saddles, bridles, halters, and rugs come in different sizes and must be bought to fit the pony.

Also important, although it's not technically equipment, you'll need to find somewhere to keep your pony. This might be a field, stable, or a boarding yard.

Here's a list of what you'll need:

Tack (stable gear)
Grooming kit
Rug
Tools for mucking out
Riding clothes
Horse trailer
Paddock and stabling

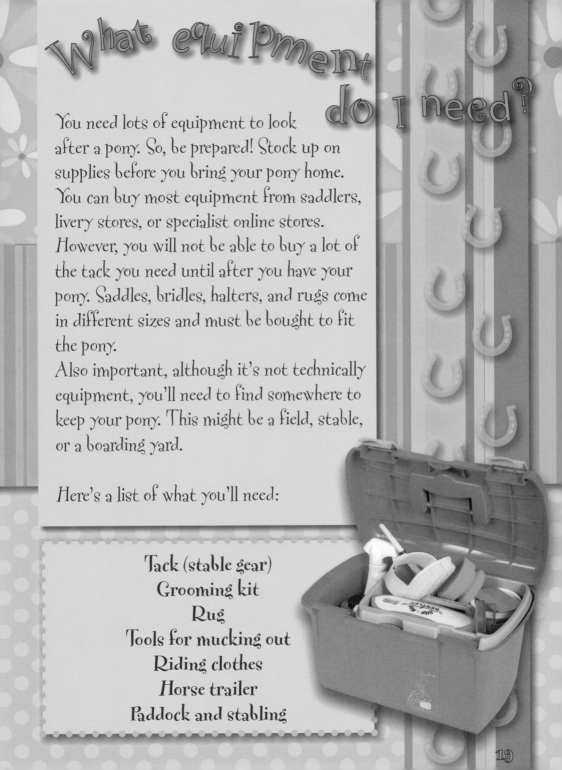

Tack

Tack is the term used for the saddle, bridle, halter, and all the equipment you need to guide and ride your pony. When buying tack, always ask the advice of an expert. Here are the basic things you will need.

Saddle Choose a well-fitting saddle that is the right width for the pony's back. The saddle is attached to the horse by a broad, smooth strap called a girth.

Saddle cloth or numnah These are placed under the saddle to keep the saddle clean and stop it from slipping.

Stirrups These are metal supports for the rider's feet. They are attached to straps that hang down on either side of the saddle.

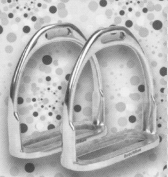

CLEANING TACK

- Wash the bit and clean mud off the bridle.
- Clean the underside of the saddle with saddle soap, but don't get the leather too wet.
- Wipe any mud off the stirrup irons.
- Clean the girth straps and stirrup leathers.

Bridle The bridle is used to control a pony when riding. It consists of leather or nylon straps that fit around the pony's head. These straps are connected to a metal "bit" that goes in the pony's mouth. The bridle should not pinch the pony's ears.

Bit The bit is the metal part of the bridle that goes in the pony's mouth. By pulling on the reins, which are attached to the bit, the rider can control the horse. The bit must be the correct size and fit.

Halter A halter is made up of leather or nylon straps that fasten around the pony's head. It is used to lead a pony or tie it up, but not for riding. Make sure it fits well.

Lead rope You need this to lead your pony to and from the field or to tie it up.

TOP TIP

When you buy a pony, ask the owner if you can buy the pony's tack and equipment. That way, you can be confident that it fits. Always check the quality, though.

Grooming kit

You will need a selection of brushes and combs for grooming your pony. The right equipment will make it easy to keep your pony clean and healthy.

Here is a list of the most useful items:

Dandy brush This is a stiff brush which is used to clean mud and dirt from the pony's body and neck area.

Body brush This is softer than the dandy brush and can be used on your pony's face and other sensitive areas. It's designed to remove dust and grease from the coat.

Mane and tail combs These are wide-toothed metal or plastic combs used for combing the pony's tail and mane.

Metal currycomb Used for scraping dirt out of the body brush when grooming.

Rubber currycomb Used to remove mud and loose hairs from the body.

22

Sweat scraper Used to wipe away sweat or water after washing.

Hoof pick A metal or plastic instrument used for removing dirt and stones from the underside of a pony's hoof.

Sponges Simple sponges or cotton wool can be used to clean the pony's eyes, nose, ears, and mouth.

Polishing cloth A damp cloth or soft sheepskin mitten will help to polish your pony's coat to a bright shine.

IMPORTANT
Keep all your grooming kit together in one bag or box. And remember to keep your brushes clean.

TOP TIP

If the tail is too tangled to get the comb through, try giving it a good brush with the body brush first.

A rug

When the weather turns cold, most ponies benefit from a warm rug.

Rugs may be made of cotton, wool, or synthetic fabrics.
The rug is held in place either by a roller, which is a strap that fits around the pony's waist, or by surcingles, which are straps attached to the rug that buckle together.
Fit the rug properly, so the pony can move freely and lie down and roll without the rug slipping forward or backward.

- An anti-sweat sheet is a kind of fine mesh rug that allows the pony to cool down after exercise without catching a chill.
- A New Zealand rug is waterproof and can be worn out in the field.
- An exercise sheet keeps the pony's back warm during exercises in winter.

TOP TIP

Lower the rug gently onto the pony, rather than throwing it over. Start at the front of the pony, then slide it into place.

Mucking out

If you plan to keep your pony in a stable, you will need to muck it out every day. This is important to keep down the risk of illness from dirty bedding.

Here's what you'll need:
- garden fork for straw bedding or a shavings scoop for wood shavings
- long-handled broom with stiff bristles
- broad shovel
- wheelbarrow
- bucket
- rubber gloves for removing manure
- rubber boots

Thunder loves mucking-out time so he can spend some time out of his stable with the other ponies. It's a good time to make friends.

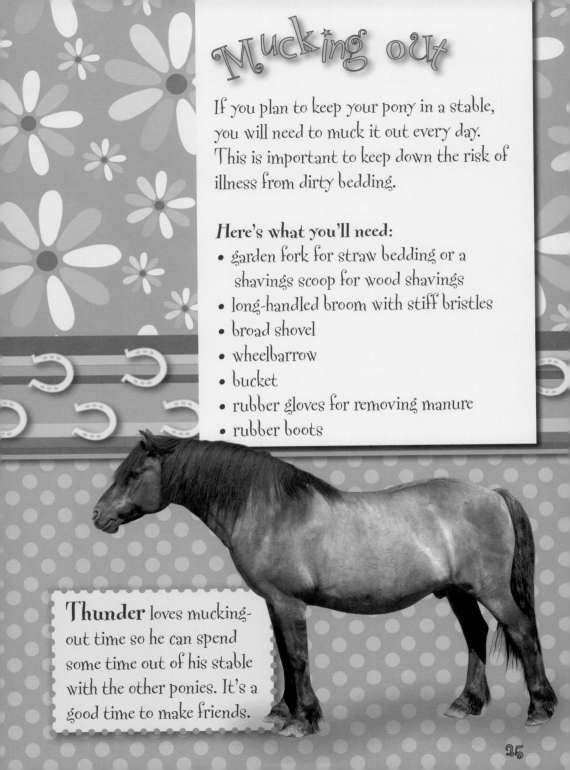

What to wear

Not only does your pony need a lot of special equipment – so do you. Many of the items of clothing you will have to buy will help keep you safe while riding. Here are some "must-haves."

- **Hard riding helmet** This must comply with national safety standards. In most countries, you have to wear a helmet by law when riding a pony. Make sure the helmet fits you and doesn't slip off. Don't cut costs – it might save your life!

- **Riding boots** These can be long or short, but must have non-slip soles and low heels so that you can't catch your foot in the stirrup if you should fall.

TOP TIP

All this gear costs a lot of money, so why not start with second-hand stuff? You can find good deals at your local stables or through your local pony or riding clubs. You can also go online with a parent to check out online auctions.

- **Jodhpurs or breeches** These are stretchy trousers that leave room for movement when you ride. Jodhpurs have long legs and are designed to be worn with short riding boots; breeches finish just below the knee and are meant to be worn with long riding boots.

- **Body protector** This is a special padded waistcoat – like a life jacket – which protects you in case of a fall. If you're going to compete in cross-country events, you'll probably have to wear one anyway, but it's worth being safe.

- **High visibility gear** If you ride on the road, wear a reflective, high-visibility vest.

- **Gloves** A pair of riding gloves will keep your hands warm and protect them from injury when leading horses.

SAFETY TIP

When riding and dealing with ponies, it's a good idea to remove all jewelry such as earrings, rings, necklaces, and bracelets as these can easily get caught and cause injury.

Traveling with your pony

If you want to take part in gymkhanas and shows, you will need a horse trailer to transport your pony and all its equipment around. Look for horse trailers for sale in the classified section of your local paper and (with a parent) on the Internet.

You will need to protect your pony during transportation; otherwise, the movement may cause it to knock its legs.

- Protect your pony's legs with travel boots or bandages.
- Bandage your pony's tail to stop it from rubbing against the back of the horse trailer.

SHOW CHECKLIST

Remember to take the following:
- Your tack, including saddle, bridle, etc., plus some saddle soap to keep it clean
- Riding clothes that you're going to wear
- Food and water
- First-aid kit

Ponies can be kept in a field, in a stable, or in both.

LIVING IN A FIELD

- Ponies, particularly tough, native breeds, are happiest in a field where they can graze freely and socialize with other ponies. It's their natural habitat.
- It's cheaper to rent a field than a stable.
- Ponies that live in a field have fewer breathing problems.
- You don't need to muck out every day.
- Muddy conditions may make it difficult to groom horses in winter.
- Ponies may need extra feed in winter.

Angel is a hardy Shetland pony and loves the outdoor life.

SAFETY TIPS

- Check that the fences and gates are strong and secure.
- There should be some kind of shade or shelter to protect your pony.
- Never use barbed wire around a pony field. It can cut the animals' legs.

29

LIVING IN A STABLE

- Most horses need stabling at least at night during the winter.

- It makes life easier to have a stable for grooming and other activities indoors during cold weather.

- If your pony is in its own stable, make sure it can see other horses. Ponies are sociable animals and may develop bad habits if they don't have company.

- It costs more to rent a stable than a field.

- Stables need to be mucked out every day.

- Ponies that are housed in a stable all year round can be prone to breathing illnesses, caused by dust in the bedding.

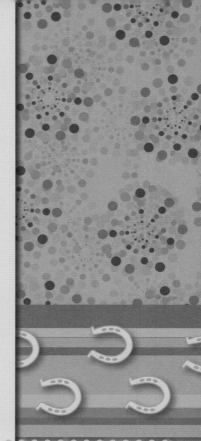

Jumper lives in a stable – but he's never lonely because he gets lots of time to run with his friends in the paddock.

TOP TIP

You'll find lists of fields and stables to rent in your local paper, on the Internet, and in horse and pony magazines.

Boarding yards

If you are new to owning a pony, it might be a good idea to keep your pony at a boarding yard. A boarding yard is a place that houses other people's horses or ponies. There are different kinds of boarding, but whichever you choose, boarding yards are expensive! You will need a lot of money to pay for your pony's food and upkeep.

Here are the main kinds of boarding:
- **grass keep** where the animals live outside
- **part boarding** where the animal is stabled at night and turned out during the day
- **full boarding** where the yard feeds, grooms, and exercises your pony
- **D.I.Y. boarding** means that the yard will house your pony, but you have to care for it and exercise it.

Frisky is kept at a boarding yard. She can go outside in the day but is stabled at night. She loves it and has made lots of friends.

31

Quick Quiz

Here's a quick checklist to find out if you've got all the stuff you need for your pony. Of course, there are some things, such as a saddle and bridle, that you can't buy until after you've bought your pony! Circle Yes or No for each item.

1. Wheelbarrow — YES/NO
2. Jodhpurs or breeches — YES/NO
3. Hard riding helmet — YES/NO
4. Field or stable — YES/NO
5. Grooming kit — YES/NO
6. Saddle soap — YES/NO
7. Rug — YES/NO
8. Riding boots — YES/NO
9. Protective vest — YES/NO
10. Horse trailer — YES/NO

How many "yes" answers did you circle?

All 10 — Wow! You are seriously prepared. You've even got a horse trailer!

7–9 — Getting there. You're pretty much ready.

4–6 — Okay, but you need to check up on the things you missed.

1–3 — Get going! You've got some shopping to do!

pony care

pony care

So, you've chosen your pony and you have all the equipment you need to look after it.

Now its time to get to work! Why? Because your pony will need all the care you can give. You'll need to spend time getting to know each other and establish a daily routine together.

Jumper is an intelligent pony and needs a regular daily routine. He is easily upset by sudden surprises.

Settling your pony in

Ponies are sensitive, intelligent animals. By nature, they live in herds, so if they suddenly find themselves on their own, away from everything they know, they can become frightened or stressed.

All of this means that your new pony might find it difficult to settle down in his new surroundings. It might take several days or even weeks before he is used to his new home. During this time you might notice some changes in his behavior. Your pony might have been calm and quiet when you first saw him, but now he is alert and lively.

Be patient! Just give your pony time to settle down and allow him to get used to his new paddock or stable.

Establish a routine. Ponies are creatures of habit and like regularity and routine.

Spend time with your pony. Your pony also needs to get to know you. Spend time reassuring him, touching him, and talking to him. Move quietly and confidently – ponies are easily scared. As you spend more and more time together, you'll soon develop a firm friendship based on trust and understanding.

If problems do develop, get help and advice from an experienced rider as soon as possible.

IMPORTANT

Don't shout and yell around your pony. Big movements and loud behavior will upset him. And try to move with confidence. If you are nervous, your pony will be nervous, too.

PONY FACT

Ponies are always slightly nervous and ready to run because in the wild, they are prey animals and could be attacked by a predator at any minute. Wild ponies live together in herds and don't like to be on their own.

Learning pony talk

Your pony can "speak" to you! But it won't use words — it will do so through its behavior. So, if you want to speak pony, you have to watch carefully.

Here are a few clues to help you understand how your pony is feeling.

- If the tail is swishing nervously, it means the pony is anxious; something is worrying him.
- If you enter a pony's stall and he turns his back on you, it means he doesn't want you there! Don't ignore this! Get out of there at once; otherwise, you might get a kick.

A pony's ears are particularly important — how your pony holds its ears will tell you a lot about what it is feeling.

How to read your pony's ear signals
- Ears relaxed, upright, facing to the side: "I'm happy and relaxed. Life's great!"

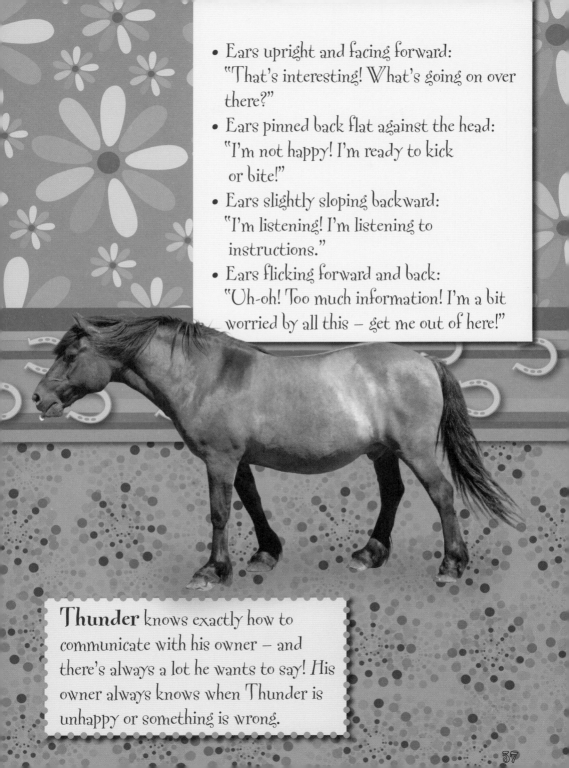

- Ears upright and facing forward: "That's interesting! What's going on over there?"
- Ears pinned back flat against the head: "I'm not happy! I'm ready to kick or bite!"
- Ears slightly sloping backward: "I'm listening! I'm listening to instructions."
- Ears flicking forward and back: "Uh-oh! Too much information! I'm a bit worried by all this – get me out of here!"

Thunder knows exactly how to communicate with his owner – and there's always a lot he wants to say! His owner always knows when Thunder is unhappy or something is wrong.

Feeding your pony

In the wild, ponies spend most of their time grazing on grass and other plants. Ponies and horses have small stomachs and large intestines, which means that they need a lot of food, but only in small portions. It's important that they don't get too much food inside their stomach at once.

IMPORTANT

- Feed little and often.
- Let the food settle – don't exercise your pony immediately after feeding.
- Allow your pony to graze in a field for part of the day if possible.
- Feed your pony at regular times.
- If your pony is in a stable, feed it some carrots or turnips for a treat.

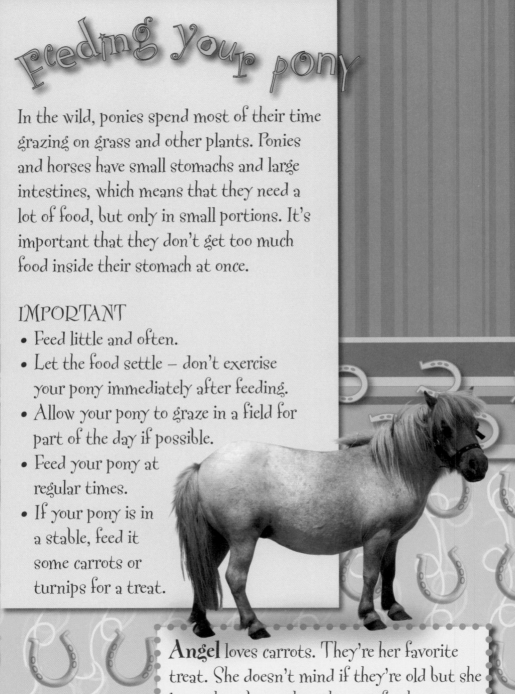

Angel loves carrots. They're her favorite treat. She doesn't mind if they're old but she loves them best when they are fresh and crunchy!

Kinds of pony food

Pony feed comes in two types: bulk feed and hard feed. Most ponies will survive on grass alone from spring through autumn, with some hard feed and hay in the winter. If you work your pony hard, it will need more energy-giving hard feed in its diet.

- **Bulk feed**, sometimes called long feed, is food such as grass or hay. This forms the biggest part of your pony's diet.

- **Hard feed** is a mixture of different ingredients that come in a hard, concentrated form such as pony nuts.

- **Mineral blocks and licks** can be used in the field or stable to make sure your pony is getting enough minerals.

IMPORTANT

Ponies love apples but don't give them too many, since they can cause colic.

TOP TIP

Feed must be kept somewhere clean and dry where rats or mice can't get to it.

How much food?

The amount of food a pony needs depends on its size, age, and type. However, the diet of an average pony should be about 70 percent bulk feed and 30 percent hard feed. Ask an expert to work out what is the right amount for your pony.

If you can see your pony's ribs sticking out, it is too thin. This may be from a lack of food, but it could also be due to illness. Ask the advice of a vet.

If your pony has thick pads of fat around the shoulders or a large belly, or if you can't feel the pony's ribs or spine, then it may be too fat.

PONY FACT

Ponies cannot vomit! This means that whatever a horse eats – oats, straw, rotten grass, or even rusty metal – must go all the way through the digestive system. This is why ponies and horses are prone to stomach upsets and colic.

Water

Your pony should have access to fresh, clean water at all times, in the stable and in the field.

Water buckets and troughs must be scrubbed clean regularly and, in winter, any ice removed at least twice a day.

In the stable, water should be put in a plastic water bucket and placed in the corner, so it won't be knocked over. Change the water often and keep the bucket clean.

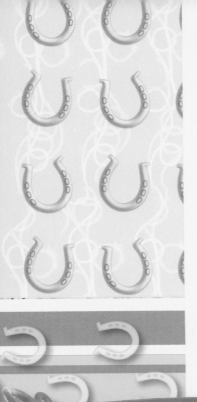

In the field, water can be supplied by a self-filling water trough. If you don't have one of these, you will need to take containers of fresh water to the field every day.

SAFETY TIP

If there is a pond or stream in your pony's field, it is best to fence it off since the water may be dirty. The edges can also get muddy, which is slippery and bad for a pony's feet.

Caring for a field-kept pony

How to make life in a field safe and happy!
- Check the pony and field twice a day.
- Remove manure from the field and shelters at least once a week.
- Do not overgroom the pony. This allows grease to build up and protect the coat.
- Inspect your pony's feet every day.
- Spend time touching and talking to your pony. Ponies love company.
- Make sure fresh, clean water is available at all times. Break the ice twice a day in winter. Clean out water troughs.

IMPORTANT
Some plants, such as ragwort, buttercups, and yew, are poisonous to ponies and must be removed immediately. They can kill.

SAFETY TIP

Every so often, ponies are stolen from their field. To be safe, get your pony micro-chipped and make sure all gates are padlocked. Never leave your pony in the field wearing a halter.

Caring for a stable-kept pony

How to make life in a stable safe and happy!

- Establish a good routine, so your pony knows when to expect its next feed.
- Make sure your pony gets enough exercise. Take her out for regular rides.
- Provide fresh, clean water at all times.
- Leave the pony out of the stable for as long as possible during mucking out.
- Don't let your pony get bored. Hang a carrot or turnip from the ceiling for her to have fun trying to catch.
- Allow your pony some time out at grass every day if possible.
- Ponies are herd animals and need company. Make sure your pony can see other horses and ponies from her stable door.

Jumper gets to spend time out at grass every day. He loves running with his friends. He also loves it when his owner spends time talking to him, grooming him, and touching him.

45

How to muck out a stable

If your pony is kept in a stable you will need to muck it out every day. This is hard, dirty work. You need to clean out all the old straw and bedding and remove all the pony manure. Dirty stables attract insects and damp bedding can cause hoof problems.

Here's how to "muck out" a stable:
- Wear old clothes and rubber gloves and boots. You're going to get dirty.
- Take your pony out of the stable. A good time to muck out is when he is out at grass. Empty the stable of water buckets and feeding tubs.

TOP TIP

Mucking out is a dirty job, so dress in suitable clothing. Horse urine and manure can ruin good leather riding boots, so change into a pair of strong rubber boots. Rubber gloves keep hands clean and dry.

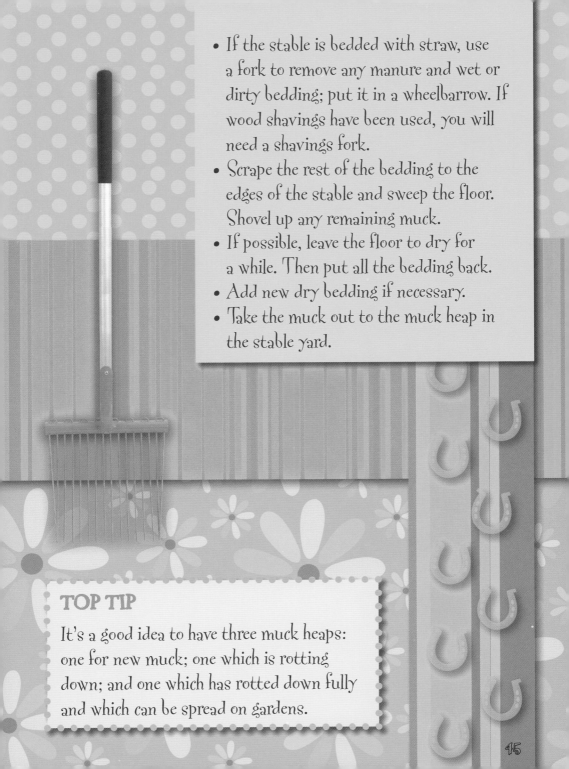

- If the stable is bedded with straw, use a fork to remove any manure and wet or dirty bedding; put it in a wheelbarrow. If wood shavings have been used, you will need a shavings fork.
- Scrape the rest of the bedding to the edges of the stable and sweep the floor. Shovel up any remaining muck.
- If possible, leave the floor to dry for a while. Then put all the bedding back.
- Add new dry bedding if necessary.
- Take the muck out to the muck heap in the stable yard.

TOP TIP

It's a good idea to have three muck heaps: one for new muck; one which is rotting down; and one which has rotted down fully and which can be spread on gardens.

How to groom a pony

A pony needs careful grooming to remove dirt and dust and keep the coat healthy and glossy. The amount of grooming you do will depend on how often the pony is worked and how hard.

Here's how to groom your pony:

- Tie your pony up securely.
- Start with the rubber currycomb. Use a gentle circular motion to loosen the dirt.
- Use the dandy brush to "flick" out the dirt from the coat. You should see a little cloud of dust with each brush stroke.

TOP TIP

Never use stiff brushes or combs on a pony's face. Ponies have very sensitive skin around their nose, and there is also the danger of damaging an eye.

- Use the body brush to smooth down the hair and get rid of excess dirt.
- Next use the mane comb to comb the horse's mane.
- For the tail, you can use a mane comb or the dandy brush. Be careful, though, as the mane comb can break the hairs.
- Use the hoof pick and a brush to clean the hooves.
- Finally, wipe the coat with a damp cloth or sheepskin mitt to bring out the shine.
- Clean the pony's face, nose, and eyes with soft sponges and cotton wool.

DID YOU KNOW?

Quartering is giving your pony a quick clean – brushing him to remove stains or shavings before going out for a ride.

Jumper loves being groomed. Not only does it keep his coat in tip-top condition, it is a good time for him to bond with his owner.

Washing your pony

Sometimes, if your pony is very muddy, you will need to give her a proper wash. Washing a pony is a bit like washing a car, only your pony will move around a lot more. So, be prepared to get wet!

- Gently hose the pony's body. Don't spray water in her face or eyes.
- When your pony is wet, gently soap her body with a soft sponge and special horse shampoo.
- Rinse off the soap. Use a sweat scraper to get off most of the excess water, but don't use it on the face or legs.
- Towel down your pony, then walk her around until she is dry.

Angel loves being washed. She stands very still, waiting patiently for the whole thing to be over. But as she's the smallest pony, it doesn't take too long!

TOP TIP

Make sure you only wash your pony on a bright sunny day so that she will dry quickly.

48

Caring for legs and feet

You need to check your pony's feet and legs every day for any signs of damage that could lead to lameness.

- Stand the pony on a level surface. Check that he is walking comfortably and that when he stands still, the weight is carried equally by all four feet.
- Check the hoof for stones and pick them out with a hoof pick. Brush off any mud.
- Check the hoof for splits and cracks.
- If your pony is wearing shoes, check that they are not twisted or loose.

SAFETY TIP

Be careful picking up a pony's foot. Slide your hand down the leg so that you do not startle or tickle him. Keep your own feet away from the pony in case he treads on you.

TOP TIP

In winter, you can apply petroleum jelly or liquid paraffin to your pony's lower legs to help stop the mud from sticking.

CARR & DAY & MARTIN

VANNER & PREST™
HOOF OIL

• For an immediate show-ring shine
• A superior, traditional ...tion

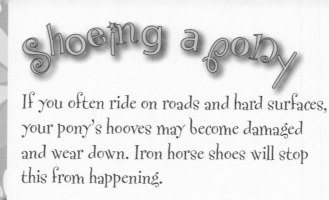

shoeing a pony

If you often ride on roads and hard surfaces, your pony's hooves may become damaged and wear down. Iron horse shoes will stop this from happening.

A pony's hooves are like fingernails. They grow continually and you need to get them professionally trimmed and balanced every six to eight weeks to keep them healthy.

The person who shoes and cares for a pony's hooves is a farrier. The farrier will travel to where the pony is kept to give advice on hoof care and shoeing. The farrier heats each metal horse shoe in a furnace. He can then hammer it into the right shape to fit the pony's foot. He then cools the shoe in water and nails it onto the pony's foot. This does not hurt the pony.

Frisky is a nightmare to shoe. She wants to be off racing around the paddock, not standing still having her toenails clipped.

After-a-ride checkup

During a ride, your pony will got hot and sweaty. So, you need to make sure that at the end of the ride you check her over and care for her, so that she doesn't catch a chill.

- Let your pony walk the last section of the ride to allow her to cool down.
- When you reach home, unsaddle your pony and give her a thorough checkup.
- Pick up her feet and check for stones.
- Check her legs for thorns and feel for any swelling.
- Get rid of any excess mud with the dandy brush.
- Put a rug on her to keep her warm. If she is wet, put a layer of straw under the rug first – this is called "thatching."
- If she is tired offer her a half-bucket of tepid water, and give her some hay to eat.

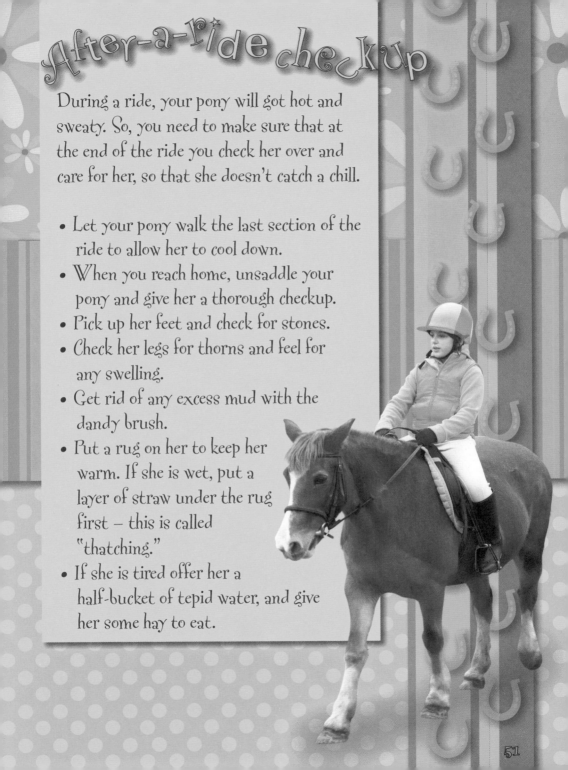

Safety around ponies

This whole section has been about caring for your pony, but these two pages sum up some of the things you can do to keep yourself safe when working with your pony. Ponies are large and often unpredictable animals, and it's important to know how to protect yourself from injury.

- Be careful when lifting heavy weights —ask someone to help you or make two trips.
- Always wear sensible clothes for riding. By law, you must wear a hard riding helmet, and a body protector is advisable, too.
- Wear fluorescent and reflective gear when riding on roads, especially in poor weather.
- Be confident with your pony. If you are nervous, your pony will be nervous, too.
- Take out insurance – called "public liability insurance" – just in case your pony hurts someone or causes damage.

CAUTION HORSE AND RIDER

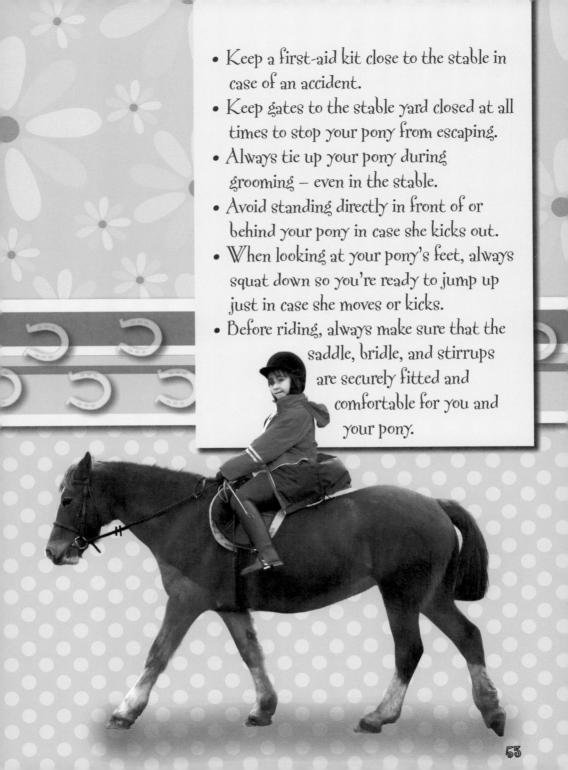

- Keep a first-aid kit close to the stable in case of an accident.
- Keep gates to the stable yard closed at all times to stop your pony from escaping.
- Always tie up your pony during grooming – even in the stable.
- Avoid standing directly in front of or behind your pony in case she kicks out.
- When looking at your pony's feet, always squat down so you're ready to jump up just in case she moves or kicks.
- Before riding, always make sure that the saddle, bridle, and stirrups are securely fitted and comfortable for you and your pony.

Quick Quiz

Test your pony care knowledge
How much have you learned about caring for your pony? Answer the following questions and find out!

1. Ponies like routine. True or false?
2. What does it mean when your pony's ears are upright and face forward?
3. What is your pony saying when he turns his back on you in the stable?
4. Ponies like big meals once a day. True or false?
5. Why is grass or hay called "bulk feed"?
6. Ponies cannot vomit. True or false?
7. How often should you muck out a pony's stall?
8. Why should you wash your pony on a sunny day?
9. How should you pick up a pony's foot?
10. What is the name of the person who shoes horses and ponies?

Answers

1. True. As prey animals, anything unusual makes them nervous.
2. There's something going on that your pony is interested in.
3. He doesn't want you there! So, get out quick.
4. False. You should feed them little and often.
5. Because it forms the biggest part of a pony's diet.
6. True. That means that a simple stomach infection can be serious.
7. At least once a day.
8. So he will dry quickly.
9. Slide your hand down the leg so that you do not startle or tickle him.
10. A farrier.

How many did you get right?

All 10 Great job. You're a top pony carer!

7–9 Good. You obviously look after your pony well.

4–6 Okay, but there are a few things you might want to check up on.

1–3 Have another read through this section of the book, then try again.

A healthy pony

A healthy pony

The better you know your pony, the more likely you are to notice if it is injured or sick. It is important to check your pony every day so that you can pick up any problems early. If you are worried, call the vet.

A normal, healthy pony will have bright eyes, a shiny coat, and a good appetite. His ears should be pricked forward and alert to different sounds, and his nose should be clean and dry.

Watch your pony. If he is fit and healthy, he will be interested in what is going on around him and will investigate what is happening. In a field with other ponies, he will spend most of his time grazing, but will also play and gallop around with his companions.

PONY FACT

Did you know horses and ponies can doze standing up? They only sleep for four to five hours a day and one usually stands guard while the others are lying and sleeping.

Knowing your pony's body

It is useful to know the names for all the parts of your pony's body. Here are the words you are most likely to come across:

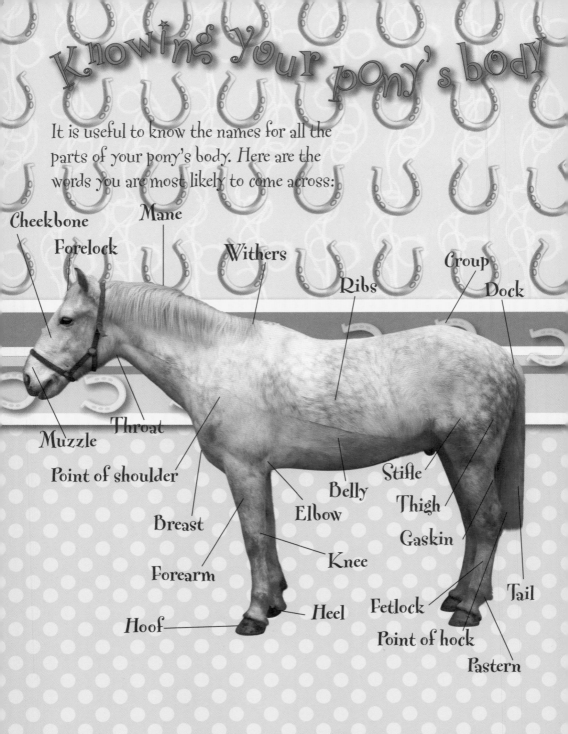

Cheekbone

Mane

Forelock

Withers

Croup

Ribs

Dock

Throat

Muzzle

Point of shoulder

Stifle

Belly

Thigh

Breast

Elbow

Gaskin

Forearm

Knee

Tail

Hoof

Heel

Fetlock

Point of hock

Pastern

Signs of ill health

Always keep checking your pony for signs of ill health. If you are worried, you should call the vet. It is often easier – and cheaper – to treat illnesses early on than to wait until they are really serious. Here are some tell-tale signs that might indicate your pony is feeling unwell.

- Your pony is standing with head drooped and looking unhappy.
- The coat is dull and in poor condition.
- She might be breathing heavily.
- If she has a cough, she might have worms or another infection.
- Shaking the head, rubbing the ears, and discharge from the ears are signs of an ear problem. It could be mites, but it could be an infection.

PONY FACT

Ponies that are kept on their own in a stable can get bored and develop bad habits, such as swaying from side to side.

57

pony health check

Here are some health care routines that you can use to check your pony's health.

- **Checking the pulse** Feel under your pony's jawbone for the pulse and count the number of beats in a minute. It should be 35–45 when he is resting.
- **Checking for lameness** Watch your pony walking and standing still on a firm, level surface.
- **Checking for leg injuries** Run your hand down the legs to check for any swelling or heat.

Ask the vet to give your pony a regular check up. He or she will be able to spot any problems and deal with the more difficult routine care tasks such as looking after the pony's teeth and checking his temperature.

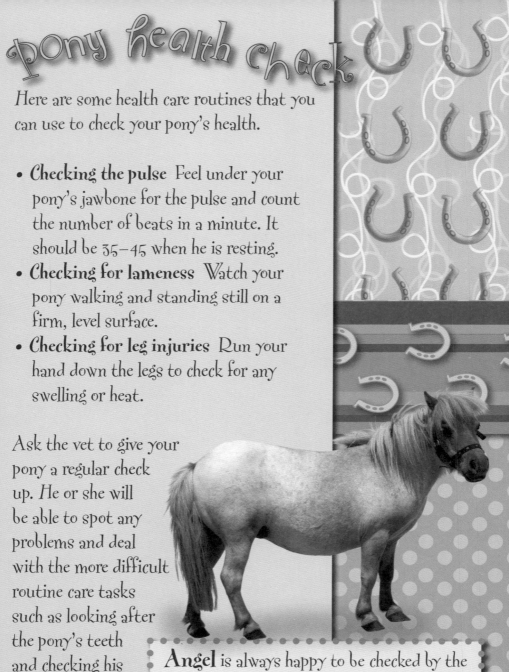

Angel is always happy to be checked by the vet. She knows what's good for her and she always wants to help.

An adult pony has between 36 and 40 teeth. Horses' teeth, unlike yours, never stop growing – so they never wear down. But as a horse gets older, its teeth can wear unevenly, and sharp edges can appear that can cut the cheeks and tongue. If this happens, a horse dentist can file them down. Your pony's teeth should be checked by a dentist at least once a year.

Signs of tooth problems:
- Lack of appetite
- Dribbling
- Sores around the mouth
- Bad breath
- Chewing slowly or on one side
- Dropping food when eating

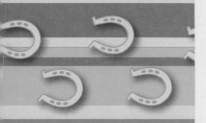

PONY FACT

Your pony's lips are flexible. A pony can't pick up food with his hooves, so he uses his lips instead. If you feed your pony a snack or treat, hold it flat on your hand and the pony will pick it off with his lips. It tickles!

Back problems

Most back problems are caused by poorly-fitted equipment, such as a saddle. However, they can also be the result of an injury, such as a slip or a fall. If you have any doubts, ask the advice of a vet.

Signs that your pony might have a bad back:
- Stiffness when moving
- Unhappy to wear a saddle
- Hollowing her back and unhappy to be ridden
- Stiffness on one side
- Bucking or bolting
- Refusal to do usual tasks
- Jumps when touched or pressed on the back

TOP TIP
All riding horses and ponies should have the fit and balance of their saddle checked by a master saddler at least once a year.

Measuring your pony

Ponies and horses are measured in "hands" (4 inches/ 10 cm). A pony is a horse that measures fewer than 14.2 hands (57 inches/ 1.4 m) high.

To measure a pony's height, first find the wither, which is the bump at the top of the neck, where the back begins (see p. 56). Measure up from the ground by the pony's front hoof to the highest point of its wither. To work out how high your pony is in hands, take this measurement in inches and divide it by four.

DID YOU KNOW?

A hand is an old measurement that is the width of an adult hand across the base of all four fingers. 14.2 hands is the same as 14 hands and 2 fingers.

Simple first aid

It's useful to know some basic first-aid
techniques that you can use to soothe
non-serious health problems and injuries.
Make sure you always have a first-aid kit on
hand when you visit your pony in case of an
emergency. If your pony is sick, in distress,
or badly injured, call a vet immediately.

- Catch, calm, or settle the pony.
- Look at the injury.
- Clean out any scratches or wounds with
  warm water and a little antiseptic. If the
  wound is bleeding a lot, call a vet.
- Hose down injured legs with cold water
  to reduce swelling and pain.
- You can treat minor cuts and scratches
  with antiseptic wound powder. This also
  helps keep flies away.

TOP TIP

Find out as much as you can about first aid
for your pony by reading a first-aid guide.
There are lots available in bookshops, online,
and in libraries.

FIRST-AID KIT

Here is a list of 10 useful items to include in your pony's first-aid kit.

1. Digital thermometer
2. Antiseptic wound cleaner for washing infections and cuts
3. Sharp scissors
4. Wire cutters in case you need to free your pony from a wire fence
5. Gauze or cotton padding to cut up for dressing wounds
6. Self-sticking bandages
7. Zinc oxide cream to protect and heal small cuts
8. Epsom salts for drawing out infection
9. Antiseptic cream or ointment to help heal cuts and scrapes
10. First-aid handbook and a notebook with the vet's number written in it

DID YOU KNOW?

Tubbing a foot means putting a pony's foot and lower leg into a bucket of warm water and Epsom salts to draw out infections from the hoof. Ask an adult to help you do this, though; otherwise, you'll have buckets of water flying everywhere!

Weighing your pony

Weighing a pony is tricky. You can't just put him on the bathroom scale!

The easiest way to find out what your pony weighs is to use a weigh band. This is a kind of tape measure marked out in pounds instead of inches.

Wrap the tape around the pony's girth, which is the area of the body about 4 inches (10 cm) behind the front legs, just behind the wither. It's like taking your own waist measurement. Then read off the measurement where the tape joins up.

PONY FACT

Most adult ponies weigh between 400 and 700 pounds (180–320 kg).

Quick Quiz

Answer these eight simple questions to find out how much you know about pony health!

1. How much does a "hand" measure?
a) 2 inches (5 cm)
b) 4 inches (10 cm)
c) 6 inches (15 cm)

2. How long do ponies sleep?
a) 4–5 hours a day
b) 6–7 hours a day
c) 8–9 hours a day

3. Your pony is shaking his head a lot. What might this mean?
a) He doesn't agree with you.
b) He wants to eat.
c) He might have an infection or ear mites.

4. How many teeth does an adult pony have?
a) 20–24
b) 25–30
c) 36–40

5. Why are ponies' nostrils so big?
a) Because they cannot breathe through their mouths.
b) Because they are related to elephants.
c) Because they rely on their sense of smell.

6. Tubbing a foot means

a) rubbing a foot with petroleum jelly.

b) putting a pony's foot and lower leg into a bucket of warm water and Epsom salts.

c) banging the pony's foot against a tub to get the mud off.

7. Hosing injured legs with cold water does what?

a) Reduces the swelling and pain

b) Cleans the mud off

c) It doesn't help at all.

8. What is a weigh band?

a) a kind of headband

b) a tape measure to read the weight of your pony

c) part of the bridle

ANSWERS

1. b	2. a	3. c	4. c
5. a	6. b	7. a	8. b

How many did you get right?

6–8 Great. You're a vet in the making!

3–5 Not bad. But there is still stuff you could learn to keep your pony happy and healthy.

1–2 Try again! Your pony needs your help!

Notes

My favorite pony

Place a picture or drawing of your favorite pony here. This could be your very own pony, a pony you love to ride, or a pony friend.

My pony's name is:

My pony's age:

Where my pony lives:

All about my pony

What kind of pony do you have?

What color is your pony?

What color is your pony's mane?

What color is your pony's tail?

What color are your pony's eyes?

Is your pony a good runner?

Does he or she love to race?

Does he or she enjoy jumping?

Is he or she friendly?

Is your pony very strong?

Is your pony quiet or lively?

MY PONY scrapbook

Use these pages to keep pictures of your favorite ponies. You can cut out news items or stories from magazines and put them here, too.

If you are lucky enough to have your very own dream pony, use these pages to keep a photo record as you grow up together.

What my pony likes

What does your dream pony like? Here you can list all of his or her favorite things. Add pictures if you want!

Favorite people:

Favorite places:

Favorite food:

Favorite pony friends:

Favorite activities:

Favorite games:

Things my pony really doesn't like:

MY pony's health record

Here's a place where you can record the details of your pony's health. Use these pages to write down visits from the vet, the farrier, and any other health professionals.

Vet's name . . . .

Address . . . .

. . . .

. . . .

. . . .

Telephone: . . . .

Mobile: . . . .

HOME VISITS

Date . . . .
Who came . . . .
Reason for visit . . . .

Date . . . .
Who came . . . .
Reason for visit . . . .

Date . . . .
Who came . . . .
Reason for visit . . . .

Date . . . .
Who came . . . .
Reason for visit . . . .

Date . . . .
Who came . . . .
Reason for visit . . . .

Horse and pony facts

- One of the first horses lived about 50 million years ago and had toes! It was called *Hyracotherium* and was only as tall as a fox. Over millions of years, it changed to become a modern horse.

- Horses and ponies have around 175 bones in their body.

- The way in which a horse moves is called its gait. A horse has four gaits: walk, trot, canter, and gallop. A gallop is the fastest gait.

- A horse's hoof is like your fingernails. It grows at a rate of about $1/5$ inch (1 cm) per month.

- A pony's leg joints are not fully fused (grown) until around the age of $3\frac{1}{2}$.

- A pony can see in two directions at once, but it cannot see anything that is directly in front of or behind it.

- Ponies make eight basic sounds — snort, squeal, greeting nicker, courtship nicker, maternal nicker, neigh, roar, blow.

- A baby horse is called a foal. A newborn foal can stand as soon as it is born.

- You can tell how old a horse is by looking at its teeth. A horse gets all of its teeth by the time it is five years old – and they never stop growing!

- Any marking on a horse's forehead is called a star – even if it's not star shaped.

- A male horse is called a stallion and a female is called a mare.

- The world's smallest horse is Thumbelina, who lives in the U.S. and measures just 17 inches (43 cm) tall – the size of a small dog!

PONY BREED LIST

There are more than 300 breeds of horse and pony. Here are just a few of the most popular pony breeds.

American Shetland • American Welsh Pony • Australian Pony • Camargue • Connemara • Dales • Dartmoor • Exmoor • Fell • Fjord • French Saddle Pony • Gotland • Hackney Pony • Highland • Icelandic Pony • New Forest • Pony of the Americas • Riding Pony • Shetland • Welsh Mountain Pony • Welsh Pony • Welsh Pony of Cob Type

pony dictionary

Arena A large outdoor or indoor riding area with sand.

Anvil A large iron block on which a farrier shapes a horseshoe.

Bareback Riding a horse without a saddle.

Bedding Soft material, such as wood shavings, shredded newspaper, straw, or sand used to line the floor of a stall.

Bit A metal bar that goes in the pony's mouth. It controls the pony while riding and is attached to the bridle.

Body brush A short-bristled brush for removing dirt from the pony's coat.

Box stall A stable where the pony is free to move about.

Bulk feed Grass, hay, or other food that forms the bulk of a pony's diet.

Chaff Chopped hay and straw, which is mixed with other feed to stop the pony from gulping it down too quickly!

Clipping Shaving off a pony's winter coat. This helps it not to sweat too much.

Currycomb A plastic or rubber comb used to remove loose hair and dirt.

Dandy brush A brush used for removing dried mud or grooming a field-kept pony.

D.I.Y. boarding Where a pony is housed at a boarding stable but the owner does all the daily care.

Dock The area at the top of the tail.

Farrier Someone trained to look after ponies' feet and put shoes on them if necessary.

Fetlock The "ankle" joint of each leg.

Field shelter An open shed in a field where the pony can find shelter.

Foal A baby pony or horse.

Full boarding Housing a pony at a boarding stable with the stable staff doing all the daily care.

Girth A strap that fastens around the belly of a pony to hold the saddle on.

Grazing Eating grass in a pasture or field.

Grooming The act of cleaning and brushing a pony.

Gymkhana A riding competition involving jumping.

Halter A leather or rope harness that fits over the pony's head and is used for leading a horse. Like a bridle without the bit or reins.

Hand The measure of a pony's height. One hand = 4 inches (10 cm).

Hard feed Corn or coarse mixes that is given to a pony in small quantities.

Hoof pick A tool with a pointed end for picking stones out of the bottom of hooves.

Horse trailer A vehicle for transporting a horse or pony.

Mucking out Cleaning out the soiled bedding and manure from a pony's stall.

Paddock A field or enclosure to hold a pony.

Pastern The part of the leg between the hoof and fetlock joint.

Pommel The front part of a saddle.

Rug A rug or blanket which is put over the pony to keep it warm.

Saddle soap Cleans and nourishes leather tack such as saddles and bridles.

Stall An indoor box where a pony is kept at times during the day or night.

Tack Equipment worn by the horse such as saddle and bridle.

Thatching Putting a layer of straw under a rug when the pony is wet.

Tubbing Putting the pony's foot in water to cure infections.

Turning out When a pony is released from the stall into a paddock or pasture.

Wither The part of a pony at the base of the neck just before the back begins.

Useful contacts

Use this page to keep a note of useful contacts, such as the farrier, horse dentist, tack shop, and stables.

Name . . . .
Address . . . .
Telephone . . . .

Name . . . .
Address . . . .
Telephone . . . .

Name . . . .
Address . . . .
Telephone . . . .

Name . . . .
Address . . . .
Telephone . . . .

Name . . . .
Address . . . .
Telephone . . . .

Name . . . .
Address . . . .
Telephone . . . .